This item was purchased with funds
donated by:

A. Sturm & Sons Foundation, Inc.

JOHN MUIR
Naturalist and Explorer

CHARLES W.
MAYNARD

The Rosen Publishing Group's
PowerKids Press™
New York

For aunts and uncles who helped teach me—Bessie and Charles, Bill, Martha, Edgar and Lile, Charlie, Allison and Phil, Sarah, Mary and Linn, Willadean and Raymond, Norma and Sam

"When I was a boy in Scotland I was fond of everything that was wild, and all my life I've been growing fonder and fonder of wild places and wild creatures."—John Muir, from *The Story of My Boyhood and Youth* (1913)

Published in 2003 by The Rosen Publishing Group, Inc.
29 East 21st Street, New York, NY 10010

First Edition

Managing Editor: Kathy Kuhtz Campbell
Book Designer: Maria E. Melendez

Photo Credits: Cover, title page, pp. 4 (bottom), 5, 7, 12 (bottom left), 15 © John Muir Papers, Holt-Atherton Special Collections, University of the Pacific Libraries © 1984 Muir-Hanna Trust; pp. 4 (top), 16 (bottom), 19 (left), 21 © Prints and Photographs Division, Library of Congress; p. 6 (top left) © Farrell Grehan/CORBIS; p. 8 (illustrated by Maria E. Melendez); p. 8 (inset) Map Division, Library of Congress; p. 11 (bottom) © David Muench/CORBIS; p. 12 (top right) © Raymond Gehman/CORBIS; pp. 16 (top), 19 (top right) © CORBIS; p. 20 (bottom right) © Bettmann/CORBIS.

Maynard, Charles W. (Charles William), 1955–
John Muir : naturalist and explorer / Charles W. Maynard.
   p. cm. – (Famous explorers of the American West)
Includes bibliographical references (p.   ).
Summary: A short biography of the man who founded the Sierra Club, from his Scottish roots to his boyhood in the Wisconsin wilderness, his travels to California, and his work as a naturalist.
  ISBN 0-8239-6291-1 (lib. bdg.)
1. Muir, John, 1838–1914—Juvenile literature. 2. Naturalists—United States—Biography—Juvenile literature.
 3. Conservationists—United States—Biography—Juvenile literature. [1. Muir, John, 1838–1914. 2.Naturalists.
 3. Conservationists.] I. Title.
  QH31.M9 M29 2003
  333.7'2'092—dc21

        2001006964

Manufactured in the United States of America

CONTENTS

The Bur-oak Shanty. Wisconsin Our first American home

Top: *Naturalist John Muir became a leader in protecting the American wilderness. A naturalist is a person who specializes in studying nature, especially animals and plants.* Bottom: *Muir made this drawing of his first Wisconsin home, a log cabin.*

John Muir was born on April 21, 1838, in Dunbar, Scotland. He was the third of eight children. John learned about nature from his grandfather as they roamed the Scottish countryside along the shores of the North Sea.

Daniel Muir, John's father, wanted to go to America. On February 19, 1849, he took three of his older children, John, David, and Sarah, to the United States aboard a sailing ship. They arrived in New York on April 5, after six weeks of travel, and made their way to Wisconsin. Daniel heard about the good farmland there. After they were settled, he sent for the rest of the family.

John (above) learned to read and spell by the time he was three years old. His grandfather, David Gilrye, was one of his first teachers. As a young boy in Dunbar, Scotland, John loved to walk in gardens and to climb the cliffs near old Dunbar Castle. John was about 25 years old when this photo was taken.

IN THE WISCONSIN WILDERNESS

Muir's invention (above) combined a clock and a desk. The clock could close up a book after a certain amount of time and bring up another and open it for Muir to study. This invention is on display today at the State Historical Society of Wisconsin in Madison.

By October 1849, Daniel Muir finished building a house on his Wisconsin **homestead**. The next month John's mother, Ann, arrived with his brother and three sisters. All the Muirs were together now. In 1855, the soil on their farm could not grow crops anymore, and the Muirs moved to a new farm near Portage, Wisconsin. They called it Hickory Hill.

John loved the wilderness around Hickory Hill. He learned the names of trees, plants, and animals. He especially liked the passenger pigeons that flew overhead. These birds, which numbered in the millions when John first saw them, became extinct in John's lifetime when the last passenger pigeon died in 1914.

John and his family worked hard on their farm. John enjoyed inventing and making objects from wood. He fashioned a wooden clock that kept accurate time. He even invented a machine that could tip him out of bed in the morning. In 1860, John took his inventions to the state fair in Madison, Wisconsin. He won a prize for his clock inventions.

Muir made this watercolor of his bed invention, which he called an early-rising machine. It tipped a sleeper out of bed when it was time to get up. Muir's inventions were well received at the 1860 state fair.

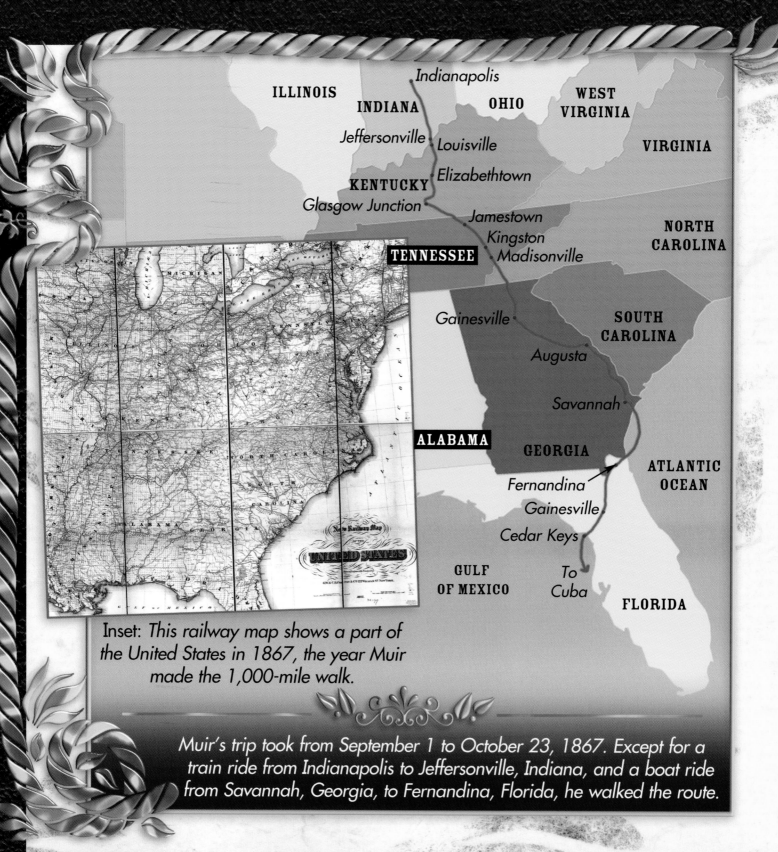

Inset: This railway map shows a part of the United States in 1867, the year Muir made the 1,000-mile walk.

Muir's trip took from September 1 to October 23, 1867. Except for a train ride from Indianapolis to Jeffersonville, Indiana, and a boat ride from Savannah, Georgia, to Fernandina, Florida, he walked the route.

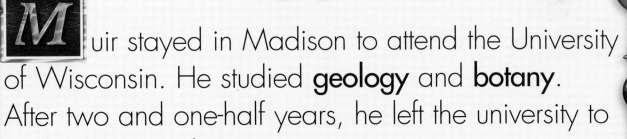

Muir stayed in Madison to attend the University of Wisconsin. He studied **geology** and **botany**. After two and one-half years, he left the university to study nature on his own.

In 1866, Muir took a job at a carriage factory. While Muir was working on a piece of machinery in March 1867, a file slipped and pierced his right eye. The injury caused him to be blind in both eyes for a few months. While he was blind, he spent time planning to go on a long walk.

After he regained his eyesight in both eyes, he set out on his journey on September 1, 1867. In his **journal** he wrote, "John Muir, Earth-Planet, Universe." His 1,000-mile (1,609-km) walk took him through Indiana, Kentucky, Tennessee, North Carolina, Georgia, and Florida. In Cedar Keys, Florida, on the Gulf of Mexico, he took a ship to Cuba.

While in Cedar Keys, Florida, where Muir boarded a ship bound for Cuba, he got **malaria**. Although he was still ill when he arrived in Havana, Cuba, he hoped to travel to South America. He wanted to explore the jungles of the Amazon. When he was unable to find a boat that was bound for South America, he went to New York. He believed he could find a boat headed to South America in New York, but he could not. From New York he sailed on the *Nebraska*, which took him to the **Isthmus** of Panama. He crossed Panama by train and then took a ship to San Francisco, California.

When Muir arrived in San Francisco in March 1868, he did not linger there. He asked a man for the quickest way out of town. The man asked, "But where do you want to go?" Muir replied, "To any place that is wild." The man pointed east. Muir crossed Pacheco Pass into the San Joaquin Valley, which was filled with blooming flowers. At the pass he saw in the distance the peaks of the Sierra Nevada for the first time. They were snowcapped and beautifully colored. Muir called the Sierra Nevada "the Range of Light."

"From the eastern boundary . . . rose the mighty Sierra . . . so gloriously colored and so radiant, it seemed not clothed in light, but wholly composed of it, . . ." Muir wrote in his book The Yosemite.

Right: *The banks of Cottonwood Creek in California's San Joaquin Valley display the natural beauty that drew Muir to this region of the country. Muir traveled through California's valleys and mountains and saw how people were destroying the land's resources. Sheep were overgrazing the meadows, and lumber companies were cutting down too many trees in the forests.*

Left: *Muir's journal is where he wrote his ideas about nature, noted observations about wildflowers, and sketched the features of the land around him.*

In the summer of 1868, John Muir reached Yosemite Valley for the first time. He was amazed at the beauty of the mountains, the waterfalls, and the river. In the summer of 1869, he returned to the mountains as a sheepherder. His job gave him time to wander and explore the mountains. Muir stayed in Yosemite in the fall of 1869. He began to explore the area as a **naturalist**, carefully making notes and sketches in his journals. On his travels he carried a blanket, a loaf of dry bread, tea, a **plant press**, his journal, and a magnifying glass. He studied the rocks of Yosemite to learn more about the valley's geology. He believed **glaciers** had carved Yosemite Valley from the mountains, which was a new way of thinking. Others believed earthquakes and water had formed the valley.

In 1874, John Muir met Louisa "Louie" Wanda Strentzel. Her family owned a large fruit ranch in the Alhambra Valley in California. Muir lived in the area while writing magazine articles about Yosemite.

John Muir married Louie Strentzel on April 14, 1880. Their daughter Wanda was born in 1881. Muir worked on his own fruit ranch in Martinez, raising grapes and other fruits. Even though Muir worked hard on his ranch, he found time each year to travel in the wilderness. Louie helped to manage the ranch, especially when John was away. The Muirs' ranch was a very successful business.

The Muirs' second daughter, Helen, was born in 1886. John took his daughters for walks in the nearby hills. He named two peaks, Mount Wanda and Mount Helen, for his daughters.

In the summer of 1884, Muir took his wife, Louie, to visit Yosemite Valley. In this letter (left), Muir described their climbing adventures and teasingly drew himself pushing Louie uphill with his walking stick.

Muir's daughters, Wanda (left) and Helen (right), often went for walks in the wilderness with Muir. Today visitors can walk on some of these paths by following the John Muir Nature Trail at the John Muir National Historic Site in Martinez, California.

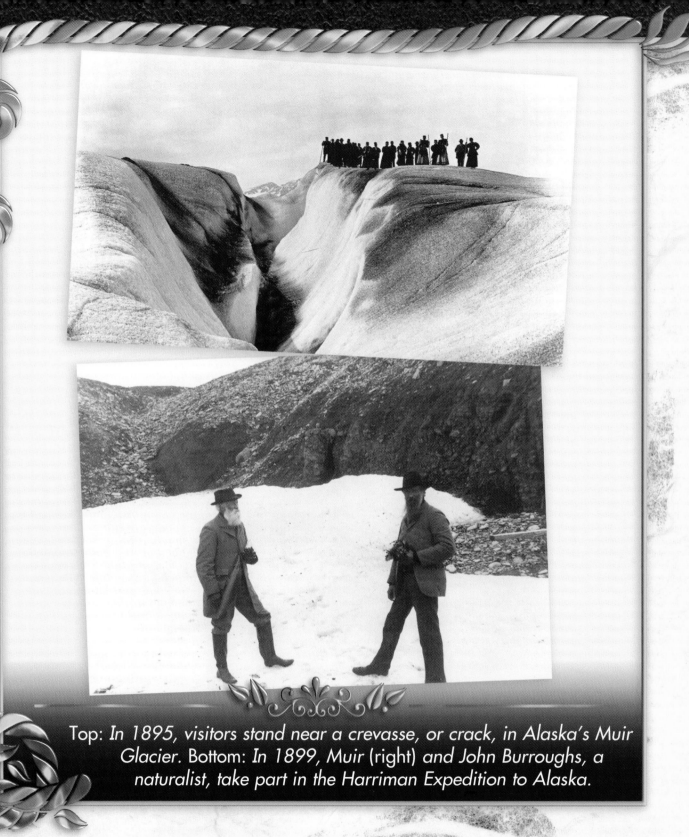

Top: *In 1895, visitors stand near a crevasse, or crack, in Alaska's Muir Glacier.* Bottom: *In 1899, Muir (right) and John Burroughs, a naturalist, take part in the Harriman Expedition to Alaska.*

Muir wanted to learn more about glaciers, so in 1879, he traveled to Alaska for the first time. There he met Reverend S. Hall Young, a Presbyterian **missionary**, who traveled with Muir on several of Muir's future Alaskan **adventures**. The two men and some native Alaskans set out from Fort Wrangell in October 1879. On this trip Muir became the first white explorer to see Glacier Bay. During this **expedition** he discovered a large glacier that was later named Muir Glacier. The native Alaskans called Muir the Glacier Chief.

Muir made seven trips to Alaska. On his second trip, in 1880, Muir had an adventure on Taylor Glacier with Reverend Young's little black dog, Stickeen. Muir later wrote a small book about Stickeen and the day they spent on the glacier.

Muir wrote about the beautiful places he visited. He penned 300 articles and 10 books. In his writings Muir described Yosemite, Alaska, and many other wild places in the United States.

In 1889, Muir took an **editor** of *Century Magazine* into Yosemite to show him the harm done to trees by lumbering and to meadows by overgrazing. Muir then wrote a series of articles asking people to save Yosemite. People all over the country became interested in saving Yosemite. In 1890, Congress made Yosemite a national park.

President Theodore Roosevelt visited Yosemite National Park with John Muir in 1903. On this trip, they camped for three days and two nights. Muir talked with the president about how to **conserve** many of America's forests and wild places.

18

Above: Muir's first book, The Mountains of California, was published in 1894. He wrote about the wild places he loved. He wanted to share his love for nature with others. In 1901, his book Our Natural Parks was published and caught the attention of President Theodore Roosevelt.

Left: President Theodore Roosevelt and Muir camped in Yosemite Valley in 1903. They are shown here at Yosemite's Glacier Point. Roosevelt later said "I shall always be glad that I was in the Yosemite with John Muir."

TIMELINE

1838 On April 21, John Muir is born in Dunbar, Scotland.

1849 John, his father, his sister, and his brother sail to New York and then travel to Wisconsin.

1861–1863 Muir studies at the University of Wisconsin.

1867 In March, Muir briefly loses his eyesight in an accident.
On September 1, Muir sets out on a 1,000-mile walk from Indiana to the Gulf of Mexico.

1868 Muir arrives in California and visits Yosemite for the first time.

1869–1872 Muir is a shepherd in the mountains of the High Sierra Nevada and then lives in Yosemite Valley.

1879 Muir makes his first trip to Alaska. He discovers Glacier Bay and Muir Glacier.

1880 On April 14, Muir marries Louie Wanda Strentzel.
In July, Muir makes his second trip to Alaska and has an adventure on a glacier with Stickeen.

1881 The Muirs' daughter Wanda is born.

1882 Muir becomes a rancher and a fruit farmer.

1886 The Muirs' daughter Helen is born.

1890 Yosemite National Park is created.

1892 Muir and his friends form the Sierra Club, and Muir serves as its president for the rest of his life.

1903 Muir camps with President Theodore Roosevelt in Yosemite.

1905 On August 6, Louie Strentzel Muir dies.

1914 On December 24, John Muir dies in Los Angeles, California.

John Muir is seen here on his Martinez ranch with his dog, Stickeen, who was named for the dog with whom he had the Alaskan adventure.

Throughout his life John Muir loved to travel. As he grew older he made trips all over the world. In 1893, he returned to Scotland, the land of his birth, and then visited other places around Europe. After his camping trip with President Roosevelt, Muir made a trip around the world from 1903 to 1904. He traveled to many countries, including England, France, Germany, Russia, Finland, Korea, Japan, China, India, Egypt, Australia, and Indonesia.

In 1911, he finally reached South America and the Amazon, and then went on to visit Africa. Muir never tired of seeing different places.

Muir guided people through Yosemite Valley to show its natural beauty. In 1871, he took the writer Ralph Waldo Emerson into Yosemite to see its waterfalls and giant sequoia trees like the one shown here. Sequoias are cone-bearing evergreens that can grow to be more than 300 feet (91 m) tall.

21

John Muir is called the Father of the National Parks because of the work he did to protect America's wild places so that others could see and enjoy them. His work and writings as a naturalist helped to establish many national parks, such as Yosemite, Grand Canyon, Sequoia, and Petrified Forest.

Muir and some of his friends started the Sierra Club in 1892, to help protect more of the Sierra Nevada. Today the Sierra Club works to save the **environment** all over the country.

Muir died on December 24, 1914, in Los Angeles, California. His legacy lives on in his books, in the Sierra Club, and in Earth Day. Earth Day, which is observed on April 21, Muir's birthday, is also called John Muir Day. It is a day to celebrate our care of the environment.

GLOSSARY

adventures (ad-VEN-cherz) Unusual or exciting things to do.

botany (BAH-tuhn-ee) The study of plants.

conserve (kun-SERV) To keep something from being wasted or used up.

editor (EH-dih-ter) The person in charge of correcting errors, checking facts, and deciding what to print in a newspaper, a book, or a magazine.

environment (en-VY-urn-ment) All the living things and conditions that make up a place.

expedition (ek-spuh-DIH-shun) A trip for a special purpose, such as scientific study.

extinct (ik-STINKT) To no longer exist.

geology (jee-AH-luh-jee) The study of rocks and their formation.

glaciers (GLAY-shurz) Large masses of ice that move down a mountain or along a valley.

homestead (HOHM-sted) A 160-acre (65-ha) tract of public land given by the government to farmers.

isthmus (IS-muhs) A neck or narrow strip of land by which two larger bodies of land are connected.

journal (JER-nuhl) A notebook in which a person writes his or her thoughts.

malaria (muh-LAR-ee-uh) A serious disease that is common in very warm places.

missionary (MIH-shuh-ner-ee) A person who teaches his or her religion to people with different beliefs.

naturalist (NA-chuh-ruh-list) A person who studies and writes about nature.

plant press (PLANT PRES) A device made up of two boards and cardboard, used to flatten and dry plants and flowers.

23

INDEX

PRIMARY SOURCES

Page 4 (top). *John Muir.* This photograph of Muir in his later years is now housed in the Library of Congress. **Page 4 (bottom).** *The Muirs' First Home, a Burr Oak Log Cabin, in Wisconsin.* The cabin was built by Daniel Muir in the summer of 1849. Muir Papers. John Muir's papers and journals are contained in the Holt-Atherton Department of Special Collections, University of the Pacific Libraries, in Stockton, California. **Page 5.** *John Muir.* This photograph was taken around the time when Muir attended the University of Wisconsin in Madison. He was in his early twenties. **Page 6.** *Muir's Clock and Desk Invention.* Muir enjoyed inventing many kinds of clock mechanisms. This one is on view today at the State Historical Society of Wisconsin. **Page 7.** *Early-Rising Machine.* This ink and watercolor illustration was done by Muir sometime after 1860 when he invented the machine . Muir Papers. **Page 8 (insert).** *New Railway Map of the United States.* This 1867 map, which was made in New York, is now in the collection of the Library of Congress. **Page 12 (bottom).** *Muir's Journal.* Muir wrote about wildflowers on this page of his journal that is now in the Muir Papers collection. **Page 15 (top).** *Letter to Muir's Family.* In this letter that Muir wrote in the summer of 1884, Muir talks about his and Louie's trip to Yosemite. **Page 15 (bottom).** *Wanda and Helen Muir.* This photograph of the Muirs' daughters was taken around 1888 in the Imperial Studio in San Francisco. **Page 16 (top).** *Muir Glacier, Alaska.* This 1895 photo shows some visitors to the Glacier Bay area. Glacier Bay was named a national monument in 1925 and a national park in 1980. Muir first visited this area of Alaska in 1879. **Page 16 (bottom).** *John Burroughs and John Muir on the Harriman Alaska Expedition in 1899.* This photo was taken during Muir's seventh trip to Alaska. **Page 19 (left).** *President Theodore Roosevelt and John Muir.* This photo was taken during their 1903 camping trip to Yosemite Valley. The photograph is now in the Library of Congress. **Page 20.** *John Muir and Stickeen.* Muir and his dog, Stickeen, are seen here on Muir's ranch in Martinez, California. His dog was named for Reverend Young's dog, Stickeen, with whom Muir had an Alaskan adventure. In 1909, Muir wrote *Stickeen: The Story of a Dog,* a popular book about the dog and the trip across a glacier.

WEB SITES

Due to the changing nature of Internet links, PowerKids Press has developed an online list of Web sites related to the subject of this book. This site is updated regularly. Please use this link to access the list:
www.powerkidslinks.com/feaw/muir/